RE-BREATHING
BUDDHA'S

FOUR
NOBLE
TRUTHS

RE-BREATHING
BUDDHA'S

FOUR
NOBLE
TRUTHS

JASON SHULMAN

Brushwork by Dairyu Michael Wenger

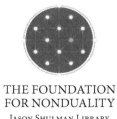

THE FOUNDATION
FOR NONDUALITY
JASON SHULMAN LIBRARY

The Foundation for Nonduality
Oldwick, New Jersey 08833
Series Editor: Nancy Yielding
Series Managing Editor: Kimberly Burnham
Editorial Counselor: Shelah Stein
Cover and Interior design: Tom Schneider
Brushwork © 2019 by Dairyu Michael Wenger
Re-Breathing Buddha's Four Noble Truths
© 2019 by Jason Shulman.

ISBN 978-0-9972201-4-8

10 9 8 7 6 5 4 3 2 1

Other works by Jason Shulman

The Nondual Shaman™: A Contemporary Shamanistic Path & Thoroughgoing Training for Awakening the Self

The Kabbalah Monographs:
    The Work of Briah
    [The Set of the World]
    The Master of Hiddenness
    The Configurations

Ecstatic Speech: Expressions of True Nonduality

The MAGI Process: A Nondual Method for Personal Awakening and the Resolution of Conflict

What does reward bring you but to bind you to Heaven like a slave? (Poetry)

The Instruction Manual for Receiving God

Kabbalistic Healing: A Path to an Awakened Soul

Four Noble Truths

1. Suffering exists

2. Suffering arises from attachment to desires

3. Suffering ceases when attachment to desire ceases

4. Freedom from suffering is possible by practicing the Eightfold Path

Preface

Jason Shulman has the voice of an ancient prophet. He is versed in both wisdom traditions and modern thought. His rhetoric comes from on top, from differentiation, but don't be mistaken: its weight comes from the hara, the belly, and integration.

I've known Jason for 52 years, since college where we both started meditating together for five minutes (a long time) with no experience of a longer sitting. We were creative and experimental. In some way, these brief meditations were our ground.

Later, we sat our first one-day sitting together. Then we sat a seven-day *sesshin* with Katagiri Roshi at the San Francisco Zen Center. After a time, our paths diverged. I moved west to study the East. He stayed in the east, immersing himself deeply in the practice all around him. Suffering has been our touchstone, and not always welcomed and appreciated by us. It's from difficulty that we learn about ease.

This book should be used as a guide, hints from one who has traveled the path, rather than an official highway atlas.

Dear Reader, meet this teaching head on. Appreciate it as well as your doubts. Suffering is a great opportunity.

Best wishes,
Dairyu Michael Wenger
Dragons Leap Temple
August 2018

Introduction

If you love the Four Noble Truths as I do, you might ask yourself *Why do we need to have these truths reinterpreted?* Or you might say to yourself *What audacity! Buddha spoke the Four Noble Truths twenty-five-hundred years ago. Why this re-breathing?* The answer is simply that the Four Noble Truths need to be breathed in and breathed out again for our age, not because they are relative truths that only depend upon the current fashion and environment, but because we have different tools now, new eyes, new populations to speak to other than the *arhats* of India in the year 500 BC and, dare I say it, new, even deeper insights that have been gathered through the hard work and good fortune of the followers of Gautama, some of whom have cleansed the Four Noble Truths of history to reveal their interior, gleaming anew. And also: we humans have a way of taking a path that is not a path and laying out its roads in concrete. We put in lighting, add road signs and lane markers—all of which is to the good. But what is then lost is the fresh and alive quality of the first utterance, along with any new insights that may have accrued.

My ultimate aim is not to present these truths as "Buddhist truths" or to harken back to some "pure" version of them, but through this new respiration, to find a way to make them pertinent in each moment of our real, actual and ongoing life. To this end, I want to look not only for received wisdom but to take wisdom at its word, the "wise-thoughts" that spring from a deep receptivity to what actually *is* rather than the thoughts that come from the imagined spiritual journey of an imagined conqueror. My aim is to help each person find the life within these truths for themselves and in this way to continue the Buddha's work. If these new perspectives contradict the way these insights have been traditionally met or what they have become by constant interaction with the confusion of all of our neuroses, then we must say together, *so be it,* as wisdom, unable to be corralled and limited, continues to gather in our hearts and minds.

Every wheel turns because it is its nature to

turn. So with the Dharma and these Noble Truths. The Four Noble Truths are a wheel in motion, a moving, dynamic, living thing that needs air and sunlight, earth and water to grow. Without these new cultivations, these truths can become obstacles instead of helpmates. These truths are meant to be handmaidens to feet-on-the-ground awakening, simple, unadorned awakening which arrives as we notice that we are innately large enough to embrace the totality of our being.

The Four Noble Truths are not meant to limit; they are not meant to be followed. They are not meant to be a structure we can judge ourselves and our attainment against. Doing this would only create shadows and constrain us to a specific type of light, one that enforces the limits of the unhealed egoic self rather than healing it into its rightful place. This type of light creates darkness around it rather than involving darkness the way Buddha did in his tea party with Mara.

I do not call myself a Buddhist any more than Buddha did, or a Christian any more than Jesus did or a Jew any more than Abraham did. All of these great ones have whispered in my ear *awake!* and I've done my best—often missing the mark—to follow their hopeful signs. When practice sits comfortably in the soul, names are beside the point.

My object in re-breathing these truths is to bring all of our disparate parts home. Without the full panoply of who we are, without a table full of our inner and outer kin, there can be no feast of truth, no thanksgiving for our perfectly imperfect human life.

This home I am attempting to find or build is not a monastery. Though often silent, it is also filled with the hubbub of human interactions, bubbling with human emotion and feeling, filled with friends, good food and cheer. And yet happily, the most profound truths can emerge in this busy home which sits in each of our hearts. In this home, no one is turned away. None of our base instincts are orphaned or rejected out of hand. None of our positive traits are idealized either. Instead, all of humanness is healed, not into some fantastical dream of enlightenment, but into something plain, ordinary, useful and helpful.

Here in this home, the good, bad and indifferent in ourselves find a way to work together for the salvation of themselves and the healing of all sentient beings. The Four Noble Truths have been an inspiration for millennia. But they must be re-breathed at every chance lest patent medicines take the place of something that illuminates because it is fresh and alive. Their fragrance awakens the fragrance already-present within each of us. These truths bring—as all real truths do—nothing new, but bring out of rough stone a figure that comes to life, a heart that begins to beat, a brain that can think rationally, and feelings that work in the service of life and not against it. This is a small book with a big heart. I hope it helps.

Jason Shulman
Oldwick/Truro 2018

Life is Suffering

Congratulations
Issa. You have
survived to feed
this year's mosquitoes.
    – Issa

The heart asks pleasure first
and then excuse from pain—
and then, those little anodynes
that deaden suffering.
    – Emily Dickenson

Freedom is only necessity understood.
    – William James

    The denial, the shame of it, the failure that it
still exists, the suffering we all hold beneath the body,
somewhere inside the bones, the feeling that we are
not in the place we ought to be, that something is

amiss, that we have missed the reason for all this *étant*, and this missing raises doubts about everything and, especially as we get older, we wonder if there will ever be this fulfillment, this place we can lie down and do nothing.

The seals are a holocaust for the fish, the fish for smaller fish, the smallest fish for plankton, the plankton for whatever it eats and whatever eats that. The whole world is mealy, granular, gritty, a graveyard for someone, some algae's son or daughter, some sun or galaxy dazzling no more but falling through everything, sliding over the surface of space, making a gravity-well that becomes its home and its coffin.

Can we hold that? Can we caress *that* the way we caress the light? The optic gives way to the... what? We use up each sense. We delight in touch until it becomes trouble at one time or another. We sniff until we become afraid of fragrance, too rich, too much body. Taste leaves us and we begin to have a sort of spiritual indigestion, bile and bitter or no taste at all, a flattening of salt, a valley of sugar. Our eyes, once joyful and alive, dim. All of this, the Buddha says, is for the good. Suffering is life's essential ingredient. Its omnipresence is almost god-like in its continuity. How horrible! Is there no escape? Endless pain from the small joint to the largest bones, young and old, from the first thought to the last. Yet, mixed within all that, bright threads on the loom along with these other things.

Are we one with the universe? Does the understanding of enlightenment cast this mixed light into everything? If this is so, then the universes—all of them—are suffering too. The beings of air, the beings that rise from the earth, Poseidon's children, the bearer of first light tied to the rock, all of the gods and bringer of goals, all suffering as they work and are worked by the world.

We arrive in space. What space are we in, with its limning lights, what book are we illuminating, what letters are we outlining in black or gold, what sentences are we compiling? When we do not know, we are lost. Even if being lost turns out to be the constant state of affairs for everything, only when we are lost and know it, can anything truly come to us. Suffering is the space of the world: it is the

first thing that makes space, that propels us out of
the uterine canal into somewhere else. Who knew
there was somewhere else? Who knew that only here
could we grow into the suffering being who could
choose, who was destined to try to choose over and
over again to be in some way that would help him
suffer less. Suffering as our teacher pointing the way
to suffering less: what a strange predicament! What
an interesting first day! The world is foam because
suffering is the lacuna, the invisible center that
allows the structure of life to be what it is. Suffering
is the signature of life and by that sign, our lost life
can be found again.

This world was born a twin, a resurrection
from the singularity of the great blankness. And so
it rises, dark next to light, star next to deep space,
happiness next to sadness, health next to illness,
god, the devil, awake and asleep, hydrogen next
to oxygen, the emptiness of space and the virtual
particles that flutter into existence out of the surface
of some invisible egg, all the opposites of the world
twinned and we beings—opposite with non-being
ourselves—selected to view all this and live in all

this, puzzled, with a mind that wants to rise above it and find a unity in which these opposites do not exist and cannot hurt us. And yet we cannot. For that is all there is, this bundle of two as the spokesman for the great unity. And we live within it, our own self shuddering on the knife's edge of oblivion. Who is there to help us?

Some have supposed that there is a part in us, let's call it a knife's edge again, that cuts the real in two and that's the problem. But we see, if we peer into the eyes of this great companion, this knife that is not an interloper, a broken organ of perception, the evil twin we think we need to erase, eradicate and renounce in order to be free, that this knife is part of who we are and we were made for this cutting as well as for joining.

Education only helps a bit and for a while, and there is no resting place unless we find a place not only for life's suffering but for the one who suffers. A place for falling asleep in Gethsemane and a place for waking up in the desert, not throwing anything away, not abandoning love for all of creation, even the troublesome parts. A place for agony in the midst of the garden. It's always like that.

Rolled into every corner of who we are and what we do, are we surprised that we search for an end to all this suffering? We are in the hospital waiting for the fever, on our arm the wristband that identifies us as someone who has been born. That is us. That is always us. Do we think we can lose who we are? Is the unsatisfactoriness of life something that is foreign to life or is it perhaps one of life's great secrets? Its engine is the primal desire for awakening that forms the core of each of us.

To view suffering as something extra, something that happens *to* us instead of *being* us, is to see it as if it had an objective existence and, having an objective existence, as something we could conquer, un-conjure, stow away, rehearse for or become accustomed to. But we are not viewing anything that is separate from ourselves. To know ourselves, to look at ourselves plainly, to realize ourselves as we truly are, is to see suffering spreading like a fertile delta, our rivers of it returning us to the source. We are made of it. All of life is incorporated with this material, braiding together our many-braided selves.

Life is suffering as the first of these noble laws
is often looked at as the thing that needs to be
swept away, the illusion that needs to be corrected
through the re-focusing of the soul, as if it were
the basic mistake that the next law and the next
would remedy and set right. But that is not correct.
Buddha's first law sets down the foundation of all
the subsequent laws, and only by seeing that this first
law is not only true but the permanent condition
of all things can we go further. Enlightenment
does not erase this condition. Unsatisfactoriness
does not disappear, though the one who felt those
things is transformed into someone who both feels
those things and simultaneously is not imprisoned
by them. Awakening is not a convenient escape
from *what-is* but the embracing of the *what-is* with
its limitations: freedom and limitation co-arising as
a single thing. The danger is that we will want to
bypass this truth and move on to something that
will deliver us. But the further laws make no sense
without seeing the continuous truth of this law. *Life
is suffering. Is. Suffering.* Without this understanding, all
of the other laws are simply the temporary escape

from this truth, and upon that flawed foundation
nothing of real consequence can be built.

To understand the nature of suffering is to be
in this time and this place without recourse to an
imaginary realm. Even the Pure Land is about
this here and now with its suffering and red dust.
A dream of non-suffering would change time and
space: no time, endless space. Where is that, exactly?
Even as we pause to hope for such a realm we lose
our connection to our true life—which is partially
personal and predominantly impersonal. Our day.
The day we are in.

And there is another twinned darkness to
complement the perceived darkness of suffering: that
of the ego's need to capture all of these noble truths
in order to create a path out of suffering that is still
under the control of the ego-as-it-is, a wonderful
portion of our psyche but one still ignorant of its
own nature, which fully believes its identity and
wants to remain unchanged, still recognizable to
itself, self-regarding and master of its own small
kingdom. Embracing suffering changes all that.
Everything modulates, morphs through contact with

the *what-is* of all this, the reagent that cuts through everything to show how to build again from the bone up.

Should suffering we can alleviate be alleviated? Of course! Do we invite extra suffering as if it were the elixir we must drink to be truly spiritual? Never! But *life is suffering* is about that fundamental current beneath everything, that existential river whose dark water waters our life's *terroir*, that never leaves and yet which can and must reveal its gifts and its catalytic power to change what cannot be changed, to bring us to the present moment with the totality of our being, to connect us to everything even as we find we are simultaneously alone and fully responsible to be who we truly are. All this comes because we are willing to see this simple truth that life is suffering and accept it fully with no escape planned by our subtle minds. Because the noble truths are four, they have a structure. Because they have a structure, they seem to exist in time. Because they seem to exist in time, the fantastic future is mixed with the problematic now. We anticipate, in other words, the cessation of suffering before we have even embraced the *one-thought-moment* of suffering as it is, neglecting to embrace each moment of time fully. Skipping over what we do not like for the end of the story, we suffer more.

These truths are not meant to be read as a narrative but as the dilemma of actual being. When Dogen-zenji says

> Firewood becomes ash; it can never go back to being firewood. Nevertheless we should not take the view that ash is its future and firewood is its past. Remember, firewood abides in the place of firewood in the dharma. Although it has a past and a future, the past and the future are cut off. Ash exists in the place of ash in the dharma.

Dogen is saying *firewood is firewood; ash is ash.* But this is not a snapshot version of reality where the linage of causality—cause and effect—is broken. In fact, it is quite the opposite: it is cause and effect in one single moment. All of the firewood's past, it seed, its tree, its growth, its cutting, its carrying and bringing forth, is in that moment. All of firewood's future is there too: warmth, cooking, eating, light and ash. All in a single pulse. This firewood is you and me, all of our birth and our eventual death, right here, right now.

It is also in the first noble truth: Life is suffering. To exist, to emerge from the background into the foreground, to arise from beings who have already arisen, who already suffer because they exist, who arose from being itself, from an atmosphere, an earth where suffering is part of creation. Only when we relate to *life is suffering* as the single, unitive state it is can we embrace the whole world, can the other noble truths come into being. Only when we embrace *life is suffering and that is all there is to it* can we embrace the origin of suffering and its cessation, a cessation that continues to move forward, that keeps being reborn because suffering continues and is born over and over again. Suffering is the nothing that destroys the established order, the zero that allows the space for something new to be born. In the *dharma*, things as they are, each thing is completely itself and in being so, illuminates the other ten-thousand things.

Suffering is the heart-breaking, heart-opening art of this world, the *chiaroscuro* of everything that moves on land or swims or speaks or is silent, of every tree and earth thing and air thing. It is the speaker within each thought, voiced or unvoiced. It is the condition of time itself that opens up a portal to suffering every second and also reveals itself in every space in the center of things or in the margin, that dissolves foreground and background, that unifies space and time, that opens the vista that has never been closed. The town and the country and all the people in each of these, all equally here on this plane of being, this light-dark place with this falling and rising up.

Life Is Suffering

The Origin of Suffering

Beings, brief, ephemeral,
Who fiercely cling to what is also passing
Will catch no glimpse of happiness
…in this life or any other.
    – Shantideva

Romeo wants Juliet as the filings want the magnet; and
if no obstacles intervene he moves towards her by as
straight a line… But Romeo and Juliet, if a wall be built
between them, do not remain idiotically pressing their
faces against its opposite sides like the magnet and the
filings… Romeo soon finds a circuitous way, by
scaling the wall or otherwise, of touching Juliet's
lips directly.
    – William James

But *why* do we cling? As I look out my window into our wild backyard, all I see is clinging. If I look closely I can see coyote and turkey trails. I've seen them, heads down, clinging nose and beak the ground, looking for food. Chromium green lichen

21

clings to the sides of pitch pines, moss to the rocks beneath, and salt, ever-present from the nearby sea, clings to my tongue. Children cling to their mothers and fathers. Our dreams cling to our daytime; our daytime thoughts cleave to our dreaming nights. With all of this clinging, why, at a certain point, does it become the origin of suffering? Why does this natural thing, built into the DNA of everything, that even fills space itself, become something we must overcome? And by what means? Through what barbiturate do we calm down a mind and body made for clinging, for this love of life that depends upon craving? I cling to my wife at night after making love. We continue and we continue. To cling and crave is to live and desire to continue living. Look at desire closely: it is growth itself. There can be nothing inherently wrong with this, and yet there it is in the second truth. Perhaps we think that we must transcend our nature, but perhaps we are mistaken. Perhaps clinging itself is not the problem or the origin of anything. Perhaps we do not completely understand why we were made. We can explore this together since we are people together, who suffer together and who want to understand all of this.

Let's call "clinging" *cohesiveness*. The body coheres. The universe is set up so that coherence—the ability of the constituent parts of any material whole—is the basis of both stability and growth. The universe grows because *things fit together*. Atoms cohere and we get molecules. Waves and particles cohere so we get light. Bell's Theorem—Einstein's spooky action at a distance—teaches us that this coherence is so important that it seems to bypass distance and time. Coherence = connection. So clinging itself, cleaving itself cannot be the problem any more than water is the fundamental problem in a potential flood or air the original problem in a hurricane.

So, our first answer to the initial question *why do we cling?* arrives. Answer: because we are made of the universe and the universe is *clinging-in-action*. The universe doesn't cling: the universe *is* clinging. There is no entity called "the universe" without the immediate mutual inseparableness of all things. The universe did not get it wrong. Since we are made of exactly the same things as the world, since we are the world and are included in the world, we did not get it wrong either. Lips to speak, to kiss, to want further and further kissing, to want to continue to exist, to survive: in this we are like everything in the universe, everything in a universe that is born and dies and thus thrives. So it seems that there is nothing inherently wrong with clinging itself. So our second question must be: *Where did our clinging go wrong?*

The problem, it seems to me, is of *identity* rather than of clinging itself. Just as the first noble truth teaches us that suffering can never disappear but that our relationship with it must change, so too clinging can never disappear since it is part of life and life is who we are. Can you picture a completely enlightened life in which clinging is still a part? Can you picture a sage-ful life in which ignorance is still present? You should be able to do that. It is salutary.

The awareness itself of awakening means that there is already a cradle prepared for awakening in us. But awakening doesn't ask us to change from who we are into something or someone else. Rather, it is really asking us to look at *identity* and see what it is made of and, in that seeing, participate in the change that occurs when our relationship to change has been refreshed and opened. The idea of awakening is a strange attractor around which a re-vivified idea can accrue. We begin to gather our lives to ourselves in new ways.

All of our life is lived in a dynamic system of interchange: our body's boundaries do not stop at our skin: we touch our environment and our environment touches—and changes—us. The oxygen in our blood is not contained solely in the tubes and tunnels of our body but extends infinitely outward. We breathe African air and Asian air and mountain and valley air. And water? Where does that start and end? We have boundaries…and we have none. When an idea of sufficient potency is dropped like a seed into this dynamic, responsive system, the system responds and changes course and grows in a new direction. We *tend toward* something new when something new, something vital and alive, is present in our living system. We gather ourselves around this thing—for good or ill.

So it is with identity. Within the [set] of identity, within the framework of that special space, everything is personal. And so it should be. We begin through the personal attraction of lovers, their histories and memories guiding their choices and actions. Then a sperm that does not speak in words but which still has its language meets an egg that also holds a world's information, and a being is born who grows into a gathering that thinks of itself as *me*, as someone, as a location in a world of places, this one closely-held place, inhabited by *myself*. What an astounding thing, the universe's constant efforts to create a *place*, a location, an identity! We don't know how stars communicate with each other, but given this strange attractor of personal-ness in this universe of tears, they must, calling out to each other in some coded language of magnetic hydrogen: *I am here. Where are you?* Everything is talking to everything.

And through this personal world, we see beauty, we innately feel the need to survive, the omnipresence of death, and the horror and glory of *being someplace*. We search for a lover, whether that lover is another person or a job or a way to be, and join in that personal effort that combines, over and over again, beauty and survival, happiness and fear. Think about it: let's go to the most elementary conditions beneath matter, the strings and harmonies of creation, and we see that they all tend toward making interactions and exchanges of influence, a type of consciousnesses that thinks or acts as a bounded infinity, a bordered thing that exists to fulfill its own destiny and makes our own!

The problem is not exactly *clinging* or *attachment to pleasure* or one of another hundred things that are described as being part of this second doorway to liberation, but rather of having forgotten that our identity *does* and *does not* belong to us, since "us" is a fiction, a momentary space created by this very assemblage of ideas and actions. *Belong* seems to be the fundamental problem, the misunderstanding of ownership. This is not a moral issue: awakening, from my perspective, does not directly address moral issues. The Buddha's laws are not moral laws so much as statements of fact about how the world works. But morality arises as an automatic outgrowth of seeing things as they are.

For some reason—need there be a reason?—life makes individuals over and over again who need to continue as persons and species, to believe that they are such things as persons, so that the program of life that includes self-consciousness goes on. The dead do not know Buddha. From this perspective, the dharmic utterances of truth are like new seeds that, dropped into this ongoing dynamic system, offer an alternative view of what is going on, one in which the closely held framework—in this case, that the world is filled with personal beings alone—is superseded by something more creative, a bigger view that includes the personal and never loses the personal, but which goes far beyond that as a definition and experience of the world.

Imagine a blind man who believes that the world is actually dark. This belief and the evidence of his blind eyes would be impossible to overturn unless something potent—let's say some new cure or a new operation—showed him that there were indeed two other things going on. First, that the world contained light as well as darkness and second, that he had an imperfection that limited his scope. So it is with identity. To deny that identity exists would be to miss its importance and beauty. That clouds of hydrogen and magnetic fields eventually help create someone who looks at suns is something that should hold awe for everyone. And yet: who does *identity belong to?* Within the limited frame of identity, the answer can only be *me.* But like the blind man cured of his blindness we must also say *identity belongs to no one.* When I think about William James' quotation at the head of this chapter, I realize that not only does Romeo love Juliet, *that* specific person, *that* one and only, but that the whole program of this attraction, unstoppable and improbable as it was, is the most *impersonal* thing imaginable: it is the universe in action, creating *more,* unstopped by Buddha or anyone's thoughts about what is moral or not, unconcerned with enlightenment or delusion. It is also not necessarily *awake.*

Traditionally, this second law has within it the understanding of identity from the perspective of its *not being true since it does not have independent existence.* It is an aggregate of conditions and things that give the illusion, so to speak, that there is a *there* there. But to me, this perspective alone is not true nonduality since it only pays attention to the deconstruction of the personal and not to its construction. It favors, in other words, one side over the other and risks equating the absolute with the world of nonduality. True nonduality *is* the *Tathagata*, the one who has gone beyond…to arrive *here*. Our idea is not to *transcend* the human condition but to *heal* it, to live it fully and consciously, to not believe the propaganda of the personal self that it is the only perspective or presence, but simultaneously to see this personal self and not attempt to turn a blind eye toward it in an attempt to avoid the pain of personal existence. There is nowhere else to go but to constantly arrive. The totality we actually live in contains the truth of this "empty" aggregation called the personal self and *also* the truth of being a personal person. To pretend otherwise would be, let us say, a shame.

From this perspective, the second law then becomes the antidote for anything that leans too far in one direction. In other words, we must understand that we are not who we pretend to be and on the other, that we will always have desire and move toward pleasure and love beauty and want to touch and see everything we can with moist eyes and lips and bodies.

We cannot transcend desire or clinging. It is only another desire that desires to do that. But we do have a chance to move to the next law and thus closer to liberation: we are all in an ark on the sea of being, our cargo and crew: everything that we are, the good and the bad, everything that is dependently co-arising, the personal *and* the impersonal, since they need each other to exist (otherwise the very law becomes inactive as we cling to the impersonal alone!) Seeing from that perspective, we realize that our freedom from every limitation is due to our very limitedness. Only then are we free to travel the high and low roads of life, to begin to ascertain how freedom makes itself known within the small [set] of our humanity, our temporary gathering into this moment in time, rising above the quantum foam for a bit, in order to take a look around.

The Cessation of Suffering

To enjoy bodily warmth, some small part of you must be cold, for there is no quality in this world that is not what it is merely by contrast. Nothing exists in itself. If you flatter yourself that you are all over comfortable, and have been so a long time, then you cannot be said to be comfortable any more. For this reason a sleeping apartment should never be furnished with a fire, which is one of the luxurious discomforts of the rich. For the height of this sort of deliciousness is to have nothing but the blanket between you and your snugness and the cold of the outer air. Then there you lie like the one warm spark in the heart of an arctic crystal.

— *Herman Melville*

To do all that we have talked about requires that we make an armistice with life. Only when the fighting has ceased—even temporarily—can we begin to create the inner space which both allows this healing into awakening to take place and simultaneously *is* that awakening itself. We form, in other words, a relationship with what actually *is*,

33

whether it is within our own self or in the world
we live in.

Sometimes this suspension of our battle with
life arises spontaneously. We hear a voice inside
our head or heart or smell a fragrance that seems
to come from someplace outside of ourselves and
we go forward on a quest to find the realization of
what we already know vaguely inside our self. Again,
more space—which is the heart of all healing and
awakening. For most of us however, this armistice—
which requires not only giving up the fight with life
and the hope of escaping our predicament, but also
asks us to walk into trouble, to counter-intuitively sit
in the path of difficulty—comes because we have
tried every possible way we could think of to suffer
less, to be relieved of our own dissatisfactions, and
found that none of them worked or worked for any
length of time. This new spaciousness then, comes
effectively from failure.

That is one way to look at it. We could also say
that that voice at the beginning or that failure to find
solace later—both of which lead us onward—are
both manifestations of exactly the same calling and

34

which some people hear sooner and some, later. Whether the speed of this hearing is encoded in our genome in the dots and dashes of amino acids or fostered by our environment and nurturance or the result of having reached bottom, only the timing is different. This voice or image, thought or feeling, is the same. The *thing-that-draws-us-onward* is the same in all cases, and the organ of that thing, that voice or thought, that Buddha-mind, is the human ego in its various guises, from integrated to orphaned, from fragmented to self-actualized. We all enter the path because we must, and it is the "impersonal's personal body" that draws us onward.

So we *turn our ear to attend*. We extend our hands to touch and, in this way, both traverse and make space. We look at the home-planet of our self and see the disturbances we carry, the balancing act we must do to keep safe, and we try to both stop the fight and watch the fight. We look for a new way. We turn our ear's unblinking, naked openness, this gyred shape that invites in whirls of sound, and are now willing to hear what is actually spoken instead of our projections based on our fear. This is why the sutras start with the words *Thus I have heard.* This mantra prepares us, gets us ready to hear what is being spoken. We need to hear the truth of suffering and its cessation. We slowly combine what we see with what we feel and what we feel with what we touch and, through the body that we will also eventually lose, find sustenance and freedom.

We could say that this third law, the cessation of suffering, has to do with the *integration of light and dark.* It is much like *shikantaza* in the Zen tradition, that whole-hearted moment of just sitting there in which we allow ourselves to experience things as they are. And lest you think "things as they are" brings forth a sort of peaceful vision of the beyond, you are mistaken. Being awake means we are aware of the totality of our being and no longer avoid the discordant truths of our origin: our life in a world of opposites. We must reckon with the truth, for example, of the actual, non-illusory existence of our personal self—our ego—and the simultaneous fact that existence itself, even the ego itself with its partial and unhealed views, *is* enlightenment… and both the cause and end of suffering. We ignore all this at our peril. If we dream it away, we float further and further away from the land we call the "other shore" but which is right here now in this moment under our feet.

Here is an example:

> *An orphan is at the door but we do not let her in. She stands silently, sometimes touching the door with soft fingers. Other times, she makes a fist. Occasionally, because things are now getting serious and the evening is getting cold, she pounds on the door. As night falls and still not invited to enter, she roars and stomps and kicks and yells. She becomes a haunting ghost, an unblinking demon, a powdered carbon that falls on everything and tints each day with its color. This is a being who cannot be transcended. This is a being, filled with desires and needs, who cannot be ignored. Our strategies—futile though they are—are few, but we try them anyway. First: Ignore her and live with her fury all night and all day. Sometimes this fury will go underground and the rejected one's voice become so distant and dim that we can convince ourselves it is no longer there, that we have conquered*

it in some way. But it is there and its rough edges, its angular shape, its echoes and negative perceptions, distort everything we do, think or feel. Its static makes life less than it is even if we have become so accustomed to it that we no longer notice its distant, disorienting hum. Or, if that strategy doesn't work: we can try to convince her and ourselves that she is not real but only an artifact created by our ignorance and that as we "evolve" we can leave her behind and trade her desire and need for a land of equanimous milk and honey. We can "grow" using our spiritual path as our escape hatch, out of our need and ignorance, our depression and mania, our fear and longing.

This is usually how we deal with the *unhealed* ego, those personal parts of ourselves that are not evolved. It has not yet occurred to us that the ego, when healed, will find its rightful place in our body, the way our hands and feet, eyes and lips find their own place as well, or that this entire vision of the spiritual path is a projection of an unreliable reporter, the unhealed ego itself.

Cessation points us continuously toward the realization of the first law: life is suffering. It does not ask us to see through suffering as if it were something we could recover from. We never recover. It does not ask us to consider our ego a mistake we can rectify by seeing it as illusion. It does not consider this world a dream. It says, essentially, that there is nothing to rise above when, from top to bottom, all of *this* is only *this*. Achievement is futile. Dreaming of a pure land without all this mess is equally futile. In our unreal dream of reality, we all want to be exempt from the first law's truth, but we cannot. This is hard news for the ego, for our sense of entitlement and accomplishment but welcomed, even by the ego, in the end. Without this realization, the ego could never heal, could never take its rightful place in our life. If life is suffering and if even clinging and desire must be embraced as part of our bedrock nature and one of the fundamentals of creation, then with the third law we begin the process of creating the Buddha-body—the one who is capable of seeing reality—and along with it, the architecture of enlightenment. This is the beginning of beauty but perhaps not the beauty we expected. Perhaps it is something much, much more.

In many people's minds, *enlightenment* has become conflated with the concept of *light* as in "filled with light." But this is terribly misleading and supports the superiority of certain aspects of reality over others, aspects chosen by the unintegrated ego who is still afraid of its shadows. So: no shadows. No unknowns. No confusions. No ambiguities. No fear. No death...and so on. What a way to bring misery to the imperfect spiritual traveler, the time-bound confused one who travels on his or her way! And what a way to cut reality down to the size the unhealed ego believes it should be! *Who is in charge here?* we must ask. In a world of uncertainty, awakening does not bring the hoped-for certainty we longed for. Mystery remains. Wildness remains. Danger remains. Vitality and freedom remain as well.

Others have redefined this term *enlightenment* in various helpful ways. One translation from the original word *bodhi* is especially meaningful to me: *to have woken up and understood.* When I wake up each

morning, as I lie in my bed with light beginning
to stream between the vertical blinds in my room,
I *understand*. Once I understood little. Now I
understand more. One day, I hope to understand
even a little more. I understand the truth of my
existing. I can feel it and know it. I understand the
omnipresence of change and death in life, life's
fragility and tenderness. I understand how lucky
I am to be in a body, to have heard the Dharma,
to have lived with enough food and money so I
could study and grow. I understand that I have had
access to medicines for my illnesses and doctors
and teachers for my soul. I understand the effect
my childhood experiences have had on my world
view, how they have influenced and often narrowed
my ability to love. I understand how suffering
comes from that and I remember all the work I've
done to rectify that. I remember, with great clarity,
the times of great light, when I palpably felt my
connection to the totality of all things and the small
dropped away in the preponderance of the great. I
remember, also with great clarity, the times of great
darkness and ignorance, illness and fear when the

small returned and the great was nowhere to be found. I see shadows and the sun and see that they can never be apart, and this joining makes of both of them something newer and more fertile. I allow dissimilarity. I allow that things do not remain as they are and that some of this happens in a darkness that is not dangerous to me but *part of me*. I remember that some things are distant and some are close, that every front has a back, that every thought and feeling has a silence around it I can trust and learn from.

Awakening due to an abundance of light is a memorable experience. But true *bodhi*, waking up, is not an experience at all, but an *understanding* that penetrates deeply into the bones and caresses the skin as well. True awakening has hands and eyes *throughout the body* as the koan says. Being one with all the experiences we have, the wave of life and even the resistance we all encounter, is our *practice-in-action*. And it is this type of practice that has no goal but the willingness itself. This is true cessation. This type of practice does not create anything. It creates everything as it allows everything to pass by

its purview. It takes everything to heart. All other
so-called cessation is purely the use of will and its
purpose is to stop the world in the hope that we can
be safe some *where*, some *place*. It is easily derailed as
life rejects its premises. Through the third law, we
come face-face with our practice, not as an idea of
what this "stopping" is, but as practice directly in the
face of life's fire. What do we awaken to? Is it only
light? Is it only clarity? True awakening—which
is true *cessation*—happens when we awaken to the
myriad things and not to some pristine nothingness.
We awake, as I have heard in the Flower Ornament
Sutra, to our delusions, to our inabilities and failures.
This is the material of waking up. This is its success.

The Finnish architect Pallasama speaks about
the homogenization of space and the loss of
ambiguity in architecture. When the space we call
enlightenment or awakening becomes homogenized,
which is to say a single thing, more of an idea than
some actual and concrete, something of the mind
alone and not the body as well, when enlightenment
becomes a *thing*, a concept, rather than a life, a thing
devoted to some idea or mode or theme, we lose

the shadow-world of participation, holding hands at midnight, the under-the-earth world that is part of our inheritance as well. In the unreal dream of enlightenment, we have annihilated difference in favor of a false version of equanimity. When we do that, we are constantly battling away all the opposites that come like orphans to bother us but who only want a home out of the rain. True equanimity exists in the company of the world. True cessation is there, too. The unhealed ego's unalloyed need for light (or really its limited concept of what light is) is really a defense against what awakening truly is. This "light" the unhealed, frightened part of us wants exclusively is the imperialist conqueror, the madman of denials of shadows and nighttime, of the fullness and odors of the ways things are. It rejects the ambiguity of every state since every state is a mixture of opposites and is boundless and bountiful. Cessation occurs when we no longer have anything to fight with since all has been invited in. This does not mean we are powerless to change things, to choose one behavior over another. Quite the contrary: the freedom to choose is the hallmark of having ceased seeing yourself as powerless, as a being who must close themselves off in fear of being found.

Is the room in the building or the building in the room? When Buddha invites Mara in for tea, where is Mara? Outside of Buddha or inside of Buddha? Only when Buddha met Mara could Buddha be completely Buddha. Tea with the enemy. Buddha does not invite Mara into his tent to evangelize Mara, to conquer Mara with kindness, or some manipulation. Buddha is not interested in having dominion over Mara. Instead, Buddha understands that he and Mara are co-dependently arising, responsible for each other as black is responsible for white. Buddha does not overcome Mara by separation but by friendship. Buddha deeply understands the intricate braiding that connects opposites throughout all dimensions.

To cease means to open the door. It means that Buddha and Mara will meet again and again not on the battlefield but over what is called in the Yiddish idiom a *glezel varmth:* a glass of warmth. It is friendship with all of reality we must depend upon. *Ceasing* is true salvation. Everything we neglect saving, everything that is not allowed its "self-ness," its existence, its difference, everything that is not met face-to-face and is not given a home in our heart-mind, can become a keening voice that bewails a lost part of our soul, standing outside of the circumference of our lives, a lost child. Or worse: an enemy whose only comfort is to conquer us.

The totality of our being includes all the beings in the Buddhist cosmology. *We* are the *devas* and formless beings, the *asuras* and *pretas* and demons, the beings of the pure and impure realms are in us, *are us.* If we speak psychologically and not iconographically, we must acknowledge that these realms are our minds and bodies. Geographically, the worlds of the *tusita* heavens and the hell realms are our bones and tissues. And, it must be remembered, so too are all the bodhisattva and Buddha realms as well. We are the place where they all have tea together. Through all of them together, and only as we see them as the entire human condition, can we lose our chains and enter the human world of limitation for that subtlest

balance of existence and non-existence, that instant
of time and no-time we call life. Entering this is
true cessation: we cease refusing to see. We cease
believing we are exempt. We cease believing we are
not limited and foolish beings. We cease believing
that there is somewhere to go to find something
that is not here. We cease by bringing our orphans
home, so that they no longer must bang on the door
at night. Doing all this, our home is peaceful and
complete.

Practice

The actions of men are the best interpreters of their thoughts.
  — James Joyce

Perhaps the truth depends on a walk around the lake.
  — Wallace Stevens

How do we remain in this country of awakening? How do we continue to grow, to not believe that we are grown once and for all? This last law, a law filled with danger, has some of the answers. This law is about the path. Was this law even written or expounded by Buddha? The Pali Scriptures say so. On the one hand, we must be grateful that a path has been laid out for us but on the other hand, this systemization of Buddha's initial insight may have been compiled later and by people other than the historical Gautama. However it occurred or was gathered, this final law is inevitable. Since we want to pass on the methodology of awakening and freedom, we are obligated to create a way, a path. What we do have to watch out for, though, is to not lose the spirit of Buddha's exploration of what freedom means and how it manifests in each of us.

What is practice? Basically, spiritual practice is a way to relate to the ego. Human beings experience their egos as the seat of their personal experience: *I felt this. I thought this. This happened to me.* As long as that perspective is true, then the spiritual path is external. Then, either we accept—or try to change—the world. In fact, when this is true, we don't actually relate to the ego so much as follow its dictates—which seem to appear in an unbidden and steady flow. The ego—this sense of selfhood that doesn't bear too much looking at, whose origins remain murky in our minds—is the invisible and often silent partner who does not even appear in relational discourse. Instead of *I think this is the way things are…* we have *This is the way things are.* In its invisibility, the ego is not seen as an editorial opinion about what it perceives but as a flashlight that illuminates what is actually there, a neutral illuminator of the way things are. Practice changes

all this. Practice changes this sense of self from
something obsidian and flint, staunch and fixed,
to something ever-changing, water petaled, cloud-
hung, forming and re-forming, spring grass and
fruit split open with rot. It brings us to the ever-
present, changing self: you cannot say it is not there,
because it is. You cannot say it is there because there
is nothing there but the field at play, no particular
self streaming its dream in real time. The Japanese
philosopher Kitaro Nishida put it best, I think, by
stating, in different words, that rather than it being
the self who has experiences, we have an experience
called "the self." It is practice and practice alone
that makes this insight possible, this tectonic shift
that gives us a new center of gravity, one we cannot
yet name but which is palpably true, its authority
earth-like in its stability and truth.

The goal of practice is impossible to achieve.
A true spiritual practice is about the failure of our
ideas and aspirations. It forces us, little by little or all
at once, to confront the impossibility of remaining
in any state we prefer. Preference is irrelevant to
practice. We never really get better at it and we

often get worse. By its length and breadth, practice constantly invites us to go beyond any experience we might have, no matter how wonderful or fulfilling it is, by showing us over and over again the birth and death of all things, the ephemeral nature of all experiences. The Buddha is talking here about practices that will challenge the very existence of the ego itself as a stand-alone element. Practice surrounds the ego in a kind of understanding that does not discard or disrespect it but which, like a new set of lenses or glasses, allows us to see this ego as one of the myriad spiritual objects, so to speak, in a world of intimately connected yet separate and identifiable objects. This type of ego does not need to be discarded as it is no longer our sole identity.

Practice is that truth in action. If we are devoted to it and continue it and accept our failure to get anywhere at all, then practice works, and we *do* get somewhere. Again: to become "expert" in a spiritual practice is to demand to be in light alone. *Partaking* of practice, on the other hand, is equal measure light and dark. It is a wonderful thing.

When we do not realize that we are having an

experience of the self, of an ego, rather than *being this ego and having an experience*, we are always separated from what we are trying to achieve. In other words, salvation (Enlightenment? Awakening?) is always *over there*, because according to the unhealed ego, there are always two worlds, one viewing the other from the distance between "me" and "not me," from what I want and what I do not have. While this is a fundamentally dissociative position, it is one we need to meet developmentally in order to grow beyond our childhood and gain agency: we are a *person* who wants certain things and can get them. But this basic one-sided view automatically brings with it dissatisfaction: the desired state is always *over there*, "not in the world we are in," and thus not within the sphere of our ego's control and temperament. In this state of affairs, there is "the world" and there is "our self," and unity depends upon how much agreement the world has with this self, how much congruency and coherency the world and other people have with the one we take our self to be. Essentially, in this position we are always some "thing" separate from the totality of life. If I am only a flower, then every winter is my enemy. If I am only snow, then spring warmth is my assassin. Change itself becomes unbearable.

Practice itself is impermanent. It is never the same twice although—especially when we are having "an experience" of light—we want it to remain and take it for "the truth" rather than an experience of a particularized moment, our editorialized moment of what enlightenment and awakening are. Practice is also primarily karmic in that it is deeply seated in the world of cause and effect. Practice accepts causation as the methodology that makes all things and, to go further, practice is causation itself. It always leads to something else. Practice lives and dies in exactly the same rhythm as life. Practice quivers and shakes. It shakes the one who does it. It is clear-sighted about life and not abstract. It doesn't indulge the conceptual but revels in the concrete. It is allied with the body and of the body. It is for the body and consequently, both eternal (though not personal) and temporary. Practice flies away with the wind. It is sometimes like lead and sometimes like air. Practice is always at

zero but whole-hearted and unworried. It sits there
inviting each of us into nothing, into someplace
where we see every problem and flaw but where
we see in the same moment the perfection of
everything, how our flaws are part of something
terrible when we ignore them and glorious as we
see the whole picture and hold our less-than-perfect
self close to our heart. Practice is tender-hearted.
Practice makes the sound of the ocean coming up
upon the shore: that strike and blast, that discharge
of energy, that quiet pat of water touching earth
over and over again and then sinking away into the
deep sands. It says *Sit down. Make the creator sit on his
foundation.* Practice is the body.

Though some may think that the actualization
of the four laws is that we step *out of* karma or
change our karma, what is actually true is that we
step *into* karma, which is to say, ride along with
karma, with cause and effect, with living and dying.
There is no other life than this one, or no other life
that should concern us. All dimensions are here.
All sleeping and awakening are here as well. All
mountain bodhisattvas and those that live in the

earth arise from here. It is *here* that has already accepted you both as you are and as the Buddha you become as you awaken to the easy and marvelous. As you build trust in your own self you can bear your untrusting moments. You do not need to conform to anything to awaken except the actual shape you make in the universe. Then, like variously shaped trees in a wonderful forest, you take your place, bent as you are by your own life, accepting more and more each day the bent and sometimes difficult shapes of others. To awaken is to enter an ecology of spirit where you are both intrinsically alone and never apart. Your ego then becomes the agency by which you interact with the world and not an impediment to love. Dare we say that word in this context? The usual wording of the four laws never includes that word. Dare we include it? Love is spaciousness and not a feeling. In its personal incarnation it does bring with it that warmth we associate with love as an emotion. But love in its largest sense is space and space is the mother of existence. We could say that love is the mother of you and me. We don't practice *in order* to be able to love: practice *is love itself,* just as it is, good and bad, filled with experiences or bereft of them, in boredom or ecstasy, with insight or blindness. If not to love, then what good is it? If not to be graceful and kind on this earth, then why bother? Love with no personal feeling is a good starting place. And it is practice that brings us there.

While it is true that awakening or enlightenment should be differentiated from experiences such as a *satori* experience or other peak moments of oneness, it is also true that these experiences serve to upset the tightly held system the unhealed ego projects upon our consciousness. It is only by the failure of such systems that we "grow weary and tired" and begin to settle down into the terrain of what is actually here. We leave some abstraction of what awakening is and enter fully into time. In other words, ideas of enlightenment as something a-temporal or eternal give way to what being time-bound actually means and how human freedom is intimately tied to the cycles of life and death. To speak personally, it took me many years to stop identifying powerful peak experiences I had during meditation with what enlightenment was. To put it simply: enlightenment contains peak experiences such as satori while satori does not contain enlightenment. There is nothing dull about an intense experience of oneness, but awakening—as an ongoing and never-finished process—is often dull!

Practice can also be looked at from these two additional angles, both of which are needed for true awakening to begin. The first is that practice is a form of self-cultivation, a way of improving ourselves and that we practice to get better at something, to achieve some goal that we believe we already have clearly in our sights. It is a way of drawing attention to our behaviors that usually go unnoticed but for the grace of practice. Practice, in this case, opens an alternative view as it simultaneously highlights behavior that is not conducive to opening the heart. In this way, practice is a challenge to the status quo of our sleepy lives wherein we only notice our self as the center of all things. Right behavior alerts us to wrong behavior. Skillful means opens us to our unskilled, unhealed, ego-bound attempts to control ourselves and others. Right view, right intention, right speech, right action, right livelihood, right effort, right mindfulness, right concentration are—from this point of view—wonderful methods of cultivating our self.

When we practice the Eightfold Path, we acquire dignity. But it must also be noted that we acquire a potential blockade toward further understanding. We might, for example, begin to believe that awakening takes place entirely—as I mentioned before—in the world of light and light's companions, such as *one* type of understanding, a *certain* type of control, a tense or "awake" consciousness, a particular kind of focus and so on. I have even seen people create speech patterns or ways of walking and dressing they believe are more "enlightened" than others. "Right enlightened behavior" takes the place of something real and alive. When we conflate the tool with its job, we run into problems. For example, in this first instance, the entire program of waking up can still easily be under the dominion of the unhealed ego since these right actions *control* the ego's behavior but do not necessarily illuminate the ego's true nature as *an experience we have* rather than an identity the self *is*. In other words, in this first use of practice, we are still within the framework of practice as something the ego *does* rather than something in which the ego participates—along with every other feature of ourselves and the universe. In this instance, the ego has been perhaps scaled and molded into something more acceptable, something finer, and certainly healed in some ways, but without the second insight into practice, the view remains small. This brings us to practice as seen from the second perspective.

In the first instance, the goal of the Eightfold Path is clear: it is the way out of suffering. Consequently, all the untamed acquisitive instincts of the unhealed ego are present. Practice is not seen for itself but for what it can bring, what it can give us. This is OK up to a point. Without the ego's desire for growth, for surcease of suffering, there would be no path. And yet, if that is all there is, awakening remains in the kingdom of behavior, and the Morning Star that so startled Buddha into sanity would remain below the horizon. *I, together with all beings, am simultaneously enlightened* only becomes a possibility when the ego passes from purely an *agency of activity*—even if it is a positive activity, as is the case in following the dictates of the Eightfold Path—to a manifestation of the already-awakened state itself.

When each piece of practice is seen as a *thing in itself*, with no demand that it be placed in a chain of causation that will lead to some nirvana as anticipated and interpreted by the unhealed parts of our bodymindspirit, then each thing, as an entity in and of itself, shows itself to be a self-illuminated existence, fully individual and yet completely connected to everything that is. It is then we wake up to see that enlightenment is not the province of the one who has awakened but the birthright of every *thing*, every atom, every sentient and non-sentient thing. Waking up simply means *we have noticed that.* This is what Dogen-zenji means when he says,

> *The mountains and waters of the immediate present*
> *are the manifestation of the path of the ancient*
> *Buddhas. Because they are the self before the*

*emergence of signs, they are the penetrating liberation
of immediate actuality. By the height and breadth of
the qualities of the mountains, the virtue of riding the
clouds is always mastered from the mountains and the
subtle work of following the wind as a rule penetrates
through to liberation from the mountains. The green
mountains are forever walking. A stone woman bears
a child by night. If one doubts the walking of the
mountains, one doesn't even yet know one's own
walking.*

With that "noticing," things begin to change.
Our behavior changes not because we are willfully
following someone's idea of what awakening is
(though that is not always a bad idea: we need more
people to follow good suggestions as to how they
act in life!) but because we see that awakening *is
already here* and that our efforts lead to our freedom
to be able to participate in this state of affairs, in
an *awakening* life. Our practice leads to conscious
choosing and to a fuller surrender to all aspects of
life, changing what we need to change and accepting
what we need to accept. Sorrow still exists. Pain and
suffering, too. And yet, there is a joy and gratefulness

that abides. It is not only the heart beating but what makes the heart want to beat. "A constant rain to benefit all beings."

Imagine, for a moment, the top of a table upon which—one by one—we place all the elements of our lives, our sorrows and triumphs, successes and failures. We can potentially place *everything that we are* on the table, meaning, in other words, with deep acceptance of the *what-is* of our lives. When we still identify with our unhealed ego as our sole personhood, however, it is the unhealed ego's editorial opinion that is in charge of what we place on this table. When the unhealed ego is in charge, there is always something we are not willing to be separate enough from to place there with other qualities our unhealed ego has deemed more acceptable, whatever they may be: our height, our body, our likes and dislikes, our various psychological states and so on.

So for example, we keep our most selfish and negative traits off the table, under a cloak of shame. To actually place these features of our lives on the table would be to bring them out into the open, to let them be seen, to see them ourselves, to have a relationship with them *just as they are*. I say *just as they are* because this table of our life has not been constructed as a therapy room, a place to gather everything that is wrong with us so we can do psychological work alone to—essentially—transcend or resolve them so that they no longer pose a threat to our sense of self. Instead, it is the place in which we can be in relationship with these situations, these descriptors of who we are as features of *what-is*. In the case of our most negative and fearful feelings, unless those eventually are placed there in front of our eyes, we never get to see their activities and distortions and instead *live them* miasmatically, spread throughout all of our perceptions, invisible to us but causing havoc nonetheless. The totality of our being is what we are after.

Finally, even when we are engaged in this most noble and difficult task of putting our whole self "on the table," we usually leave one thing out: our ego itself which we almost do not notice and which sits offstage someplace without showing itself in our consciousness. Since we are still identified with *being that* instead of *experiencing that,* this ego remains in its unhealed, which to say separate, split-off, state. Awakening is not doing away with the table or clearing this table of everything or, selectively, of all the things we do not like. It is—to the contrary— the ability to *add* to the table the totality of our self as we continue to discover our depths, our hidden positive and negative features. In this final case, it is our sense of identity as proposed by the ego itself that goes on the table, leaving us thus free to see our self as something that *contains* an ego but is not that. We begin to see how we manipulate reality by keeping this zone of the personal sacrosanct and separate, orphaned from its real home.

Then we become aware of our delusions, no longer either protecting ourselves from them or acting them out. Then we can heal what is possible to heal and there is much that can be healed once it is seen in this way. In a sense, this is a way of poverty, so to speak, one in which we see how little of our self belongs to our self and how much we really are once we begin this part of the journey as a being who is made up of the world in all its ends and beginnings, its half-finished sentences and startling statements and never-ending silences. Then, full of incompleteness ourselves, we can relate to every other incomplete being. We are the one who has conquered and yet yearns, who sees themselves as the carrier of imperfection but perhaps not the one who passes on those imperfections so freely. Our freedom then is to be limited, which is to say, real. Our freedom is to have given up dreams of being insularly safe from the turning of the greatest wheel, the wheel of life. To the awakening one—whenever he or she can remember!—each tree is the tree of life, each current is life's current, each sky *our* sky. We revel in blue and touch red and brown and yellow. We taste—when we remember!—sweetness and salt, sour and bitter.

Awakening is always *awakening-in-action* and not *awakening-as-display*, which is a sort of splendid repose that everyone sees but that helps no one and does nothing. *Awakening-in-action*, however, recognizes all the Buddhas around us and treats each one—sleeping or awake—with dignity and care, determined to be as kind as possible in this fleeting world.

These four laws are memory devices, the heart's mnemonics that thrill us every time we remember them. They thrill us not so much because they give us a rigid path but because, in an opposite way, they are the fresh and still alive moment of someone who went before us and did this work in the dark as well as the light, in the known as well as the unknown, and whose spirit and example is always there (we can feel it) saying *Remember.*

About the Author

Jason Shulman is an American spiritual teacher whose original work springs from his Judaic and Buddhist background. He is the founder of *A Society of Souls: The School for Nondual Healing and Awakening,* based in the United States, Denmark and the United Arab Emirates. There he teaches the distinctive body of nondual work he has developed to awaken the human spirit: Nondual Healing, Impersonal Movement, the Work of Return and Nondual Shamanism™. Jason's main concern has been to develop paths of healing the mind, body and spirit based on his own understanding of the difficulties inherent in the human condition. Through his studies and practice, Jason has developed a unique perspective on human consciousness and the nature of existence. His work seeks to translate this perspective into a replicable and clearly-delineated path for other seekers of truth to follow. He has been especially interested in applying personal spiritual work to methods of transforming society at large. To that end, he has created the MAGI Process, a nondual method of working with conflicts between people, institutions and governments. He is the author of numerous monographs and books, and several albums of his work as a singer and songwriter. More about his work can be found at www.societyofsouls.com and www.nonduality.us.com

About the Artist

Dairyu Michael Wenger is a Soto Zen priest and a disciple of Sojun Mel Weitsman. He has practiced Zen for 46 years, 38 of them at the San Francisco Zen Center. At the age of 63 he founded his own temple, Dragons Leap, emphasizing Zazen and brush painting; courage, compassion, and creativity.

Made in the USA
Monee, IL
01 October 2021

79121226R00046